GW00501421

LIVERPOOL
100

TRANSWORLD PUBLISHERS
61–63 Uxbridge Road, London W5 5SA
A Random House Group Company
www.transworldbooks.co.uk

First published in Great Britain
in 2014 by Bantam Press
an imprint of Transworld Publishers

Created and compiled by Will Brooks and Tim Glynne-Jones with Mike Kiely
(Liverpool) copyright © Will Brooks and Tim Glynne-Jones 2014

Design by David Ashford

Visit www.100nil.com for more indefensible screamers.

Will Brooks and Tim Glynne-Jones have asserted their right under the
Copyright, Designs and Patents Act 1988 to be identified as the authors of
this work.

A CIP catalogue record for this book
is available from the British Library.

ISBN 9780593074596

Addresses for Random House Group Ltd companies outside the UK can be found
at: www.randomhouse.co.uk
The Random House Group Ltd Reg. No. 954009

The Random House Group Limited supports the Forest Stewardship Council®
(FSC®), the leading international forest-certification organisation. Our
books carrying the FSC label are printed on FSC®-certified paper. FSC is the
only forest-certification scheme supported by the leading environmental
organisations, including Greenpeace. Our paper procurement policy can be
found at www.randomhouse.co.uk/environment

Typeset in Flama

Printed and bound in Germany

2 4 6 8 10 9 7 5 3 1

LIVERPOOL
100

UNITED
0

Created and compiled by
Will Brooks and Tim Glynne-Jones

with Mike Kiely

BANTAM PRESS

LONDON · TORONTO · SYDNEY · AUCKLAND · JOHANNESBURG

LIVERPOOL FOOTBALL CLUB

from the city of
Liverpool

MANCHESTER UNITED FOOTBALL CLUB

from the city of
Salford

Boot Room

The mark of a great manager is winning trophies. But the mark of a great club is continuing to win when that manager steps down. United's collapse after Alex Ferguson's retirement was a rerun of their embarrassing fall from grace following the retirement of Matt Busby
. . . and in stark contrast to Liverpool, where the Boot Room kept the good times rolling from Bill Shankly to Bob Paisley to Joe Fagan to Kenny Dalglish.
That's the way to run a football club.

2–0

Flying Boot Room

Ferguson's infamous flying boot
leaving David Beckham parading his
head wound for the world's press is
just one example of his management
style. Fergie regularly fell out with
respected players, put referees under
pressure, banned journalists from
Old Trafford and blanked the BBC
for seven years because they dared
asked questions about his football
agent son.

Bob Paisley (as ever) was a class
above the Scot. Rather than aim a
football boot at his left-back, he
declared pithily: 'They shot the wrong
bloody Kennedy.'

3–0

Talking of Humour . . .

LIVERPOOL XI	UNITED XI
Arthur Askey	?
Ken Dodd	?
Jimmy Tarbuck	?
Stan Boardman	?
Craig Charles	?
Faith Brown	?
Alexei Sayle	?
Les Dennis	?
Ricky Tomlinson	?
Derek Nimmo	?
John Bishop	?

Can anyone think of any famous comedians who support United? Draw your own conclusions.

Laugh at United

> **SINGING SECTION**
> PLEASE FEEL FREE TO SUPPORT
> YOUR TEAM IN THIS AREA

Spontaneous wit isn't the Mancs' forte, which
is why their fans have to have the club print
their banners for them and a 'singing section'
rubber stamped by the board.
Remember the 60s photo showing a
policeman laughing at the humour from
the Kop? And the genius banners like 'Joey
Ate The Frogs Legs, Made The Swiss Roll,
Now He's Munching Gladbach'?
It's different at Liverpool.

Newton Who?

Saturday 12 October 1895, Anfield, Division Two

Liverpool **7**
Bradshaw 2, Becton 2, Geary 2, Ross

v

Newton Heath **1**
Cassidy

Liverpool are bouncing back from relegation while the railway workers that would become Manchester United are a season into a 12-year stretch in the Second Division.

Anfield is treated to a thrashing that remains the biggest margin of victory between the clubs to this day, with goals from Thomas Bradshaw, Frank Becton, Fred Geary and Jimmy Ross adding the seventh. Joe Cassidy's goal for United can't even be called a consolation.

United hope to airbrush this embarrassment out of their history by masquerading under the name Newton Heath.

World Class City

UNESCO saw fit to grant World Heritage Status to Liverpool for the splendour of its waterfront edifices, and its year as European Capital of Culture in 2008 saw tourists flocking to the city in droves. Hard to fathom why Salford Quays never got the same attention.

Perm v Spam

What would Bobby Charlton have given to be able to grow the classic Liverpool perm, rather than labouring with the funniest hairstyle in football history? Scouse wigs sell by the hatful, comb-over wigs, less so.

Bum Fluff

What is it with United and facial hair? Maybe it doesn't grow in the rain. From Gordon Hill to David De Gea, they've struggled to cultivate anything more than a few pubescent whisps. And what exactly was that Gary Neville was trying to grow on his top lip for all those years?
When it comes to the Zapata look, Graeme Souness and Terry Mac sported 'taches worthy of toasting with a tequila.

Who's the Scouser in the Wig?

Speaking of hair, we're still chuckling about the 'Rooney weave', apparently fashioned from the trimmings of David de Gea's 'beard'. The word is it makes him more attractive to the over-60s.

10–0

Sweet FA

Wednesday 16 February 1898, Anfield,
FA Cup round two

Liverpool **2**

Dunlop, Cunliffe

v

Newton Heath **1**

Collinson

As far as the FA Cup is concerned, it's first blood to Liverpool. Following a 0-0 draw at Bank Street, the replay sees full-back Billy Dunlop and centre-forward Daniel Cunliffe do the damage.

Bad Boys

Luis Suarez takes a
nibble of Ivanovic
10 MATCHES

Eric Cantona starts a fight
with a spectator
9 MONTHS

First to Do the Double

1986
1994

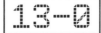

Poor Relations

It must be tough living in the shadow of your wealthy neighbours, especially when your debts run to £700million.
Over on Merseyside, there's no disputing who's the biggest club in town.

14-0

Magnificent Seven

Wednesday 25 March 1908, Anfield, Division One

Liverpool **7**
Hewitt 2, McPherson 3, Robinson 2

v

United **4**
Bannister, Turnbull, Wall 2

Having finally settled on a name, United are sweeping all aside on their way to the title, scoring fours, fives and sixes, and they rattle another four past Liverpool on this midweek night at Anfield. Thrilling stuff, except no one is paying much attention. They're far more interested in the seven Liverpool are scoring, as Charles Hewitt, Billy McPherson and Bobby Robinson fill their boots.

The Twelfth Man

'I love it here. This is what you play football for. As a young kid, I used to come to European nights and dream of playing in front of this crowd.'
STEVEN GERRARD, LIVERPOOL CAPTAIN

'I don't think some of the people who come to Old Trafford can spell football, never mind understand it.'
ROY KEANE, MANCHESTER UNITED CAPTAIN

16–0

Liquid Asset

THE RIVER MERSEY

a wonder of the natural world
that people sing about.

River Mersey

THE SHIP CANAL

a man-made blot on the
landscape that people
dump trolleys in.

Trophy Haul

41
39

Most successful English team ever? Let's count trophies, shall we? With five European Cups, three UEFA Cups, seven FA Cups and eight League Cups to add to their titles, Liverpool are still sitting proudly on their perch, despite all Fergie's efforts.

18--0

Gatecrashers

United **3**
Homer, Turnbull, Wall

v

Liverpool **4**
Goddard 2, Stewart 2

The winter of 2010 sees United move from their Bank Street ground to a brand new stadium at Old Trafford, Salford. And who should be their first opponents but Liverpool, on their way to a runner-up spot in the League. It's United who show first, pumped up with adrenalin and determined to christen the new ground in style, and they roar into a 2-0 lead. But in the second half, Liverpool fight back with two goals apiece from Arthur Goddard and James Stewart to clinch a 4-3 win that paves the way for many more joyful outings to the Theatre of Dweebs.

19—0

Big Ron – From Old Swan – Signs On

The most popular t-shirt at Anfield in 1986 proclaimed the demise of local boy-turned-United manager Ron Atkinson, who lost his job after throwing away a 10 point lead at the top of the table and finishing fourth. And who were champions again that year? Liverpool.

'He Hates Scousers'

Presumably that includes Ron Atkinson, the Scouser who managed their FA Cup winning sides in 1983 and 1985? And Steve Coppell, the Scouser who still holds the club record for most consecutive performances by an outfield player? And that chubby bald Scouser they're reputed to be paying £300,000 a week?

21-0

Food for Thought

World famous Scouse

a delicious medley of root
vegetables and lamb.

Eccles Cake

an obscure piece of patisserie that resembles
dead bluebottles in a pastry case.

22-0

1, 2 . . . 1, 2, 3 . . . 1, 2, 3, 4 . . .

Saturday 19 September 1925, Anfield, Division One

Liverpool 5
Forshaw 3, Chambers, Rawlings

v

United 0

Only goal average, two places and Bolton Wanderers separate the two clubs at the end of the season but there's a gulf in class when Liverpool welcome United a few games in, and wave them off with their heaviest defeat of the century at Anfield. Dick Forshaw is prolific this season, scoring 29 goals in 35 appearances, and he opens the scoring in the 21st minute. Harry Chambers makes it two after half-time, before Forshaw notches two more for his hat-trick and Archie Rawlings completes the rout four minutes from time. Easy.

Fox in the Box

Take a look in the Anfield Directors' Box and there's lovely Linda Pizzuti, wife of owner John W Henry and the fresh faced embodiment of a vibrant, forward thinking ownership model. Meanwhile, over at Old Trafford, they've got the Glazer boys. Well, at least there's absolutely no doubt that Malcolm was the daddy.

Peek-a-Boo

Former Liverpool chairman David Moores may have once sported the mullet and 'tache of a successful German porn star but up the M62 (no euphemism intended) Martin Edwards was living the dream, accepting a police caution for allegedly spying on the toilet habits of ladies at a Cheshire leisure club.

Anthem

When the Kop sings *You'll Never Walk Alone*, the world stops and listens. Do United even have an anthem? Does anyone know what it is? Is it *Glory Glory Man United*? No, can't be, they nicked that from Spurs. Is it *Che Sera Sera*? They only sing that when they're going to Wembley, which isn't very often these days. *Ferguson's Red and White Army*? Oh no, he's gone. *Cum On Feel the Moyes*? Oh no, so has he. It's a struggle. No wonder the place is so quiet these days.

Busby's Aces

Saturday 21 November 1936, Old Trafford,
Division One

United **2**
Thompson, Manley

v

Liverpool **5**
Hanson, Eastham, Howe 3

United spent most of the 1930s in the Second
Division, but they popped their heads up in the
First just in time for this lesson from a Liverpool
team featuring one Matt Busby. Alf Hanson
and Harry Eastham set the ball rolling half way
through the first half, then Fred Howe takes over
with a hat-trick that gives Liverpool their record
victory at Old Trafford and ultimately contributes
to another relegation season for the Mancs.

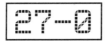

Captain Fantastic

Manchester may claim
Matt Busby as its own
but the Scot had already
achieved legendary status
prior to World War Two
– as skipper of Liverpool
Football Club.

Top-Flight Football

1962
1975

Liverpool have enjoyed an unbroken run
in the First Division, latterly the Premier
League, for 13 years longer than United.

Classic Four-Pointer

Saturday 23 November 1963, Old Trafford,
Division One

United **0**

v

Liverpool **1**

Yeats

The late, great Bill Shankly knew the importance
of small margins. At the end of this season, four
points would separate champions Liverpool
from runners up United, and that four-point gap,
which gave Shankly his first title as Liverpool
manager, could be traced back to this game.
There was quality all over the pitch and on the
managers' benches, but in the end it was one
goal that decided it, a header from Ron Yeats, his
first goal for Liverpool Football Club.

30-0

El Beatle

When the international press needed to find a
nickname for George Best after a United game
against Benfica, they turned to Liverpool for
inspiration. Well, it was either that or Herman's
Hermits. El Hermit. Mmm, catchy.

31–0

KENNY DALGLISH 102

ALEX FERGUSON 7

We're talking international caps.
While Ferguson was given a run out in 1967
but not retained, King Kenny clocked up the ton,
making him Scotland's most capped player.

First to Reach a
European Final

1966
1968

Better Than the 'Best'

United **1**
Best

v

Liverpool **2**
Lawler, Hunt

Matt Busby's United are reigning champions and less than eight weeks after this fixture they will become European Champions. Can they impose their class on Liverpool?

No.

George Best gives them the lead early on but by the 18th minute Liverpool have fought back and got the game won, thanks to goals from Chris Lawler, pouncing to stab a Ron Yeats header over the line, and Roger Hunt waltzing through the United defence to side-foot past Alex Stepney. Not only does the win prove that Liverpool are better than supposedly the best team in Europe, it also costs United the title by two points.

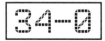

BILL SHANKLY
12

MATT BUSBY
8

When it came to international caps, Shankly had
the advantage over his United counterpart.
(Figures include official and wartime matches.)

Bullet Dodged

Lou Macari chose chip shops over championships when he opted for United over Liverpool, but to no great regret. As Shankly said: 'I only wanted him for the reserve team.'

First Domestic and
European Double

1973
1999

From Shankly with Love

Saturday 22 December 1973, Anfield, Division One

Liverpool **2**

Keegan, Heighway

v

United **0**

United's record over the festive season in 1973 makes amusing reading. Played 6, Won 1, Drawn 1, Lost 4. In fact, their whole season is a laugh-a-minute, ending in relegation, six years after winning the European Cup. Liverpool, by contrast, are champions and shaping up to be the dominant force in English football for years to come, spearheaded by 'a lad called Keegan'. But this will be Bill Shankly's last game against United. Fitting then that Kevin Keegan should open the scoring and Steve Heighway, another Shankly master-signing, should finish the job.

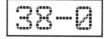

Upset

Tommy Docherty's United were supposed to be the force that was coming to challenge Liverpool in the 70s, but their first shot at glory went horribly wrong. Firm favourites for the 1976 Cup Final, they lost 1-0 to Second Division Southampton, a goal from the late Bobby Stokes doing the damage. Liverpool have never lost a major domestic cup final to lower league opponents.

39–0

1977

A big, big year in United history. They fluked an
FA Cup win over Liverpool.
The Reds had to settle for the League
Championship and European Cup.

40–0

Doc Struck Off

Back in the days when Liverpool were winning the title seven times in nine years, United had a brief moment of glory when they beat Bob Paisley's men in the 1977 FA Cup Final. It was supposed to herald the return of United as a genuine force in English football. They had an exciting young team and a charismatic manager, Tommy 'the Doc' Docherty, who was going to end Liverpool's supremacy.

But before the new season could even get under way, the Doc was struck off. Why? He'd been shagging the team physio's wife. He was replaced with the uncharismatic Dave Sexton and so began a further 16-year wait for the title, while Paisley, Joe Fagan and Kenny Dalglish won eight more for Liverpool in the next 12 years.

41–0

Boxing Day Beating

Tuesday 26 December 1978, Old Trafford, Division One

United **0**

v

Liverpool **3**

Kennedy, Case, Fairclough

Liverpool, European Champions for a second successive year, are forced to spend Boxing Day at their poor relations' up the road. It takes just five minutes for Ray Kennedy to pop the Christmas balloons and Jimmy Case grabs a second 20 minutes later. David Fairclough completes the rout, helping Liverpool to become champions again, 23 points ahead of ninth-placed United.

42–0

Advertising Space

1979

When the marketing men realized they could get good return on investment by sticking their brand name on a football shirt, the shirt they all wanted was Liverpool's. Hitachi won the race, a full four years before Sharp saw any value in United's shirt.

1983

43–0

Back to Back

Not only have Liverpool won the European Cup more times than United, they've also achieved a feat that only Nottingham Forest among English clubs can match: they've retained it. Following the European Cup triumph in 1977, a Kenny Dalglish goal against FC Brugge in the 1978 final saw the trophy remain at Anfield. United have never come close to retaining the European Cup.

44-0

Deadly Duos

From Keegan & Toshack to the SAS, via Rush & Dalglish, Liverpool have spawned a dynasty of strikers whose names go hand in hand. Hughes and McClair? Cole and Sheringham? Forlan and Van Nistelrooy? Rooney and Van Persie? Not so much.

Bruce Almighty

Wednesday 7 April 1982, Old Trafford, Division One

United **0**

v

Liverpool **1**
Johnston

In a season that ushered in three points for a win and bid farewell to the great Bill Shankly, United were actually looking like title candidates for a while. Liverpool needed a win at Old Trafford to put some distance between themselves and United, but more importantly to move two points clear of Ipswich Town. It didn't look good when United were awarded a penalty after just seven minutes but Bruce Grobbelaar saved the spot kick from Frank Stapleton and Liverpool took the three points with a Craig Johnston goal midway through the second half.
Champions. Again.

46–0

Midfield Maestros

	Souness	Robson
League Title	5	2
European Cup	3	0
Cup Winners' Cup	0	1
FA Cup	0	3
League Cup	4	1

The clash of the midfield enforcers. Well, it wasn't really a clash at all, was it? Every time 'Captain Crutches' went in for a challenge his shoulder popped out. Essentially a lightweight pumped up on Guinness, raw eggs and more Guinness, Robbo was no match for Souey, Liverpool's engine, who could tackle like a juggernaut but had the grace and guile of a cat. Their record speaks for itself. While Robbo was patched together just long enough to get one hand on the Premier League trophy in 1993 and 1994 – after 12 years of trying and failing – it was a poor return compared to Souness, who had spent his career at Liverpool winning the big honours, averaging two major trophies per season.

Classy Cameos

Graeme Souness and Sammy Lee made a fleeting but memorable appearance in Alan Bleasdale's BAFTA winning raw social commentary of the 1980s, *Boys from the Blackstuff.* David Beckham's cameo in *Goal 2: Living the Dream* was never going to have the Coen brothers knocking on his door.

48-0

15 Minutes of Hurt

Saturday 26 March 1983, Wembley Stadium,
League Cup Final

Liverpool **2**
Kennedy, Whelan

v

United **1**
Whiteside

A Norman Whiteside goal after 12 minutes
has underdogs United dreaming of an historic
League Cup and FA Cup double. But with
15 minutes to go, Alan Kennedy sends Gary
Bailey sprawling with a long-range strike
into the corner of the net, and with the game
heading towards extra time, Ronnie Whelan
curls a shot exquisitely past Bailey again, to
shatter United's dream and send Bob Paisley,
in his last major final as Liverpool manager,
up the steps to collect the League Cup for a
third season in a row.

The Treble

1984

United bang on about 1999, but Liverpool completed a European and domestic treble 15 years earlier: European Cup, League Championship, Milk Cup. And if you're talking about feats of endurance, Liverpool played two games more during their treble campaign.

1999

Great Danes

	Jan Molby	Jesper Olsen
League Title	3	0
FA Cup	3	1
League Cup	1	0

Though teammates in the Danish side of the 80s, it's fair to say Olsen was less than half the man that Jan Molby was.

The Lost Goal

Industrial action meant terrestrial TV cameras
never covered the Liverpool v United Milk Cup
clash in November 1985, when Jan Molby ran
from his own half, beating half the opposition
before hitting a screamer from outside the box.
Molby joked he had a video cassette of it in his
loft but wouldn't show it. However, it recently
surfaced. The best ever between the two sides?
Judge for yourself – it's on YouTube.

'You'll Get More Sense From Her.'

Three days after April Fool's Day in 1988 and
Fergie was still acting the red-nosed clown.
Speaking to a radio interviewer after a 3-3 draw
at Anfield, Fergie was in the middle of moaning
that visiting managers 'have to leave here
choking on their own vomit, biting their tongue,
afraid to tell the truth', when Kenny happened by,
carrying his daughter Lauren.
'You'd be better off talking to my baby daughter,'
he told the reporter. 'She's only six weeks old but
you'll get more sense from her than him.'
Fergie's reply is not recorded.

Michael Knighton

Just that name alone is enough to settle any argument with the Mancs. Not even Tom Hicks with his Liverpool embossed cowboy boots embarrassed himself to the extent of juggling a ball on the pitch before a match in the hope of getting the fans 'onside'.

54-0

Barnes Stormer

Sunday 18 March 1990, Old Trafford, Division One

United **1**
Whelan og

v

Liverpool **2**
Barnes 2

Liverpool on their way to the title, United on their way to finishing sixth. Alex Ferguson is forced to hail a 'superb' John Barnes, whose brace secures a simple win on the road for Kenny Dalglish's rampant reds. Liverpool even have to score the home side's goal for them.

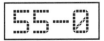

They Played For Both Sides

PETER BEARDSLEY

Beardo was one of the cleverest players English football has ever seen and one of the most successful players of his generation, but all that could have been different – he could have been a United player.

In actual fact, he was a United player – for one match, a 2-0 win over AFC Bournemouth in the League Cup. That was in 1983. Four years later, Kenny beat Fergie to the punch and signed him for Liverpool as a replacement for himself. He didn't disappoint. As well as supplying the bullets for John Aldridge, Beardo scored 59 goals in 175 appearances, won two League titles and the FA Cup and played 59 times for England. Oh, and he scored a hat-trick against United in a 4-0 drubbing at Anfield in 1990.

56-0

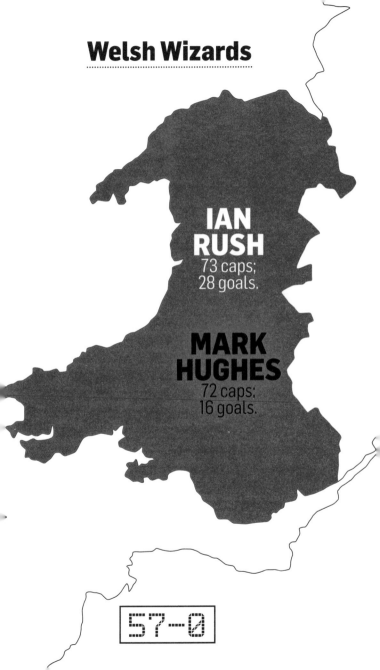

Welsh Wizards

IAN RUSH
73 caps;
28 goals.

MARK HUGHES
72 caps;
16 goals.

57–0

Beardo Blitz

Liverpool **4**
Beardsley 3, Barnes

v

United **0**

A month after drawing 1-1 in the Charity Shield, FA Cup winners United come to the home of the champions and find there is no more charity on offer. For some reason they take the field dressed in what appears to be a shower curtain. It doesn't wash. Peter Beardsley shows Alex Ferguson what he's missed out on with a hat-trick that begins in the 11th minute and finishes in the 81st with a typically deft lob. Before that John Barnes has scored the third with a header and Liverpool are left still waiting for Fergie to knock us off our perch.

European Super Cups

Famous Fans

LIVERPOOL	UNITED
Nelson Mandela *(ANC)*	Enrique Iglesias *(TWAT)*
Pope John Paul II *(Roman Catholic)*	Terry *(Christian)*
Dr Dre *(rap)*	Mick Hucknall *(crap)*
Kim Cattrall *(Sex and the City)*	Angus Deayton *(sex with a hooker)*
Mike Myers *(Yeah baby!)*	Morrissey *(miserable now)*

League Cup

No wonder United are lagging behind, it took
them until 1992 to get their first. By that time,
Liverpool had won it four times.

61–0

Chumpions

Sunday 26 April 1992, Anfield, Division One

Liverpool **2**
Rush, Walters

v

United **0**

For the first time since 1967 United are genuine title contenders. But going into this penultimate game of the season, they've just lost two games on the spin and must win at Anfield to keep their title hopes alive. They don't. Ian Rush and Mark Walters expose their frail nerves and the title goes to Leeds. Shame.

Collared

Sunday 1 October 1995. Eric Cantona is making his return for United after a nine-month ban for kung-fu kicking a fan at Crystal Palace. All eyes are on the fiery Frenchman with the turned-up collar to see if he can behave himself for a change and not get wound up. Enter Neil 'Razor' Ruddock, uncompromising stopper and renowned wit, who is marking Cantona for the afternoon. First challenge: a deft manoeuvre by Razor to turn down the famous Gallic collar. Eric manages a smile. A couple of full-blooded challenges for the ball, then Razor turns down the collar again. Eric swings at him. The third time Razor does it, Eric turns round and says, 'Me and you we fight in the tunnel!'

63-0

Three-Goal Start

Tuesday 4 January 1994, Anfield, Premier League

Liverpool 3
Clough 2, Ruddock

v

United 3
Bruce, Giggs, Irwin

The away contingent are rubbing their hands after 23 minutes as the visitors race into a three-goal lead. They think this is it – the moment they 'knock Liverpool off their perch' once and for all. Two minutes later, Nigel Clough thumps one in from 30 yards. Then he adds a second seven minutes before half-time and the away section goes strangely quiet. But have Liverpool got enough to complete the comeback? Yes they have. With 11 minutes left, Neil Ruddock lays the ball out left to Stig Inge Bjornebye and powers into the box to dominate Gary Pallister and head Bjornebye's cross past Peter Schmeichel. Keep knocking.

Top Scorer

IAN RUSH
346 goals

BOBBY CHARLTON
249 goals

Charlton is United's all-time leading goal-scorer with an average of a goal every three games, but Ian Rush outscored him by 97 goals in 98 fewer games, at a rate of more than one in two.

Club Philosophers

*'Some people believe football is
a matter of life and death . . .
I can assure you it is much, much
more important than that.'*
BILL SHANKLY

'Football – bloody hell!'
ALEX FERGUSON

Sleighed

Sunday 17 December 1995, Anfield, Premier League

Liverpool **2**

Fowler 2

v

United **0**

Eight days before Christmas, Fergie is in typically festive mood as he decks his team out all in grey for the United fans' seasonal treat – a trip to a proper football ground. For the second time in nine months, Liverpool treat their hosts to a Sunday roasting, and this time it's Robbie Fowler doing the carving with a late goal in each half.

67–0

Double Failure

Sunday 19 March 1995, Anfield, Premier League

Liverpool **2**
Redknapp, Bruce (og)

v

United **0**

Another impressive Double for United – losing two competitions at the death. In one of the dullest FA Cup finals in history they lose 1-0 to Everton, having finished second in the title race, one point behind Kenny Dalglish's Blackburn Rovers. And this game contributes greatly to their downfall. Despite going the rest of the season unbeaten, they can't make up the deficit suffered after Jamie Redknapp's first-half strike and a late Steve Bruce own goal send them home from Anfield empty-handed.

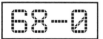

19th Century Wisdom

'THE LIVERPOOL GENTLEMAN AND THE MANCHESTER MAN'

Some things haven't changed despite the passing of two centuries.

Shades of Grey

Losing 3-0 at half-time against Southampton in 1996, Ferguson blamed the team's grey kit. Having changed for the second half, United still lost 3-1.

Thirteen years later, Liverpool players had no trouble seeing each other when they turned up at Old Trafford in all grey. It turned out to be yet another gloomy day for the locals, 4-1 this time.

70-0

Men in White

Yes, we know. But those suits in '96 were still preferable to looking like a team of Scottish accountants. Wonder who chose those?

71-0

Bad Boys *Part II*

Luis Suarez insults
Patrice Evra
8 MATCHES

Rio Ferdinand misses
a drugs test
8 MONTHS

Nice One, 'Charlie'

Wednesday 5 May 1999, Anfield, Premier League

Liverpool **2**
Redknapp, Ince

v

United **2**
Yorke, Irwin

Another glorious comeback, this time featuring former darling of the Stretford End Paul Ince. Dwight Yorke and Denis Irwin have given United a two-goal lead and with just over 20 minutes to go, Alex Ferguson must be dreaming of a win at Anfield. Jamie Redknapp pulls one back but the seconds are running out when Ince, who has been branded a 'big-time Charlie' by his former manager, lives up to his billing and forces the ball home two minutes from time to ruin Ferguson's night.

73–0

Balmy Nights in
Barcelona

United's late show at Camp Nou against
Bayern Munich in 1999 may have been
Ferguson's finest hour, but when it comes
to winning there against Barcelona, there's
only one British team that's achieved that.
And not once, but twice. 1-0 in the 1976
UEFA Cup semi-final and 2-1 in the 2007
Champions League.

74-0

BOB PAISLEY 3

ALEX FERGUSON 2

European Cups, that is. And just to rub it in, the only time Ferguson got to test himself against Liverpool outside domestic competition was as manager of Aberdeen in the 1980/81 European Cup. He took on Bob Paisley's all-conquering Liverpool team at Pittodrie and lost 5-0.

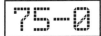

Men of the People

While Busby and Ferguson happily accepted a pat on the head from the establishment, Shankly and Paisley didn't need knighthoods, preferring the recognition of the people that really count.

76--0

Dan-Buster *Part I*

Sunday 17 December 2000, Old Trafford, Premier League

United **0**

v

Liverpool **1**

Murphy

A tight first half is creeping towards the interval when Liverpool are awarded a free-kick 20 yards from goal. Up steps Danny Murphy, who curls a peach of a strike past the wall and into the net, scraping the post on its way in. The Stretford End falls strangely silent and they never quite find their voice again after their half-time pies.

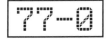

Cup That!

Liverpool won the League Cup and FA Cup in 2001, a cup double that United have never achieved. They reached the final of both in 1983, but Liverpool stopped them in the League Cup.

78–0

Dan-Buster *Part II*

Tuesday 22 January 2002, Old Trafford, Premier League

United **0**

v

Liverpool **1**

Murphy

A midweek thriller is drawing to an indecisive conclusion when Steve Gerrard chips a through ball into the path of Danny Murphy, who flicks it cheekily over Laurent Blanc and Fabien Barthez to win the game for Liverpool for a second season running.

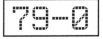

'Wrong One. Moyes Out.'

Moyes may have been clueless but hiring a plane to tow that banner over Old Trafford was a spectacular own goal. Want to know the right way to get rid of a failing manager? Anfield, December 2010: 'Hodgson for England,' sang the Kop. He didn't last much longer than that year's Christmas decorations.

80–0

Oh Brother!

The Da Silvas, the Nevilles,
the Greenhoffs . . . Liverpool players don't
need their siblings to hold their hand on the
pitch. It just goes to show you don't even
have to be the best player in your family and
you can still get a game for United.

81—0

Great Uruguayans

LUIS SUAREZ
31 goals in
37 appearances
(2013/14)

DIEGO FORLAN
0 goals in
18 appearances
(2001/02)

Forlan regaled the English press with tales of how he had tried to persuade Luis Suarez to join United. He failed to mention that Suarez would have little trouble bettering his 17 goals in three seasons at Old Trafford. It took him nine months to score his first League goal. Suarez scored three times as many in the same period.

Cardiff Cakewalk

Sunday 2 March 2003, Millennium Stadium,
League Cup Final

Liverpool **2**
Gerrard, Owen

v

United **0**

Cup wins don't come much easier than this
little walk in the park in Cardiff. Steven
Gerrard sets it up with a nice strike off David
Beckham that loops over Fabien Barthez,
giving us the joy of watching United huff and
puff for 47 minutes before Michael Owen puts
them out of their misery with a breakaway
goal four minutes from time to win the cup for
the second time in three years.

Euroflops

United's record in Europe is one of consistent failure. From 38 European campaigns, only four have been successful. Outside the Champions League, a solitary Cup Winners' Cup win over Barcelona represents their only other European knock-out success. Liverpool, from one more campaign, boast twice as much silverware, with three UEFA Cup triumphs and five European Cups.

Dan-Buster *Part III*

Saturday 24 April 2004, Old Trafford, Premier League

United **0**

v

Liverpool **1**

Murphy

United's hopes of winning the title are hanging
by a thread but a win at home to Liverpool will
keep them in the race. Can they hold their nerve?
Have they got what it takes? Do they have the
players to rise to the challenge?

No.

Cometh the hour, cometh Danny Murphy – for
a third time in four seasons – tucking away a
penalty just after the hour mark to send the
away end rejoicing again.

Welcome to Manchester

There have been one or two players that
Liverpool supporters would have been more than
happy to provide with a personal limo service to
the doorstep of another club, but turning up mob-
handed at Rio Ferdinand's house demanding
'Sign your f***ing contract'?
Not very neighbourly.

'Veni, Vidi, Vidic'

'I came, I saw, it rained'
read the banner in recognition of the Serb's disdain for the mill town's world renowned miserable climate. 'In England they say that Manchester is the city of rain,' he said. 'Its main attraction is considered to be the timetable at the railway station where trains leave for other, less rainy cities.'

87–0

'Rafa's Cracking Up . . .'

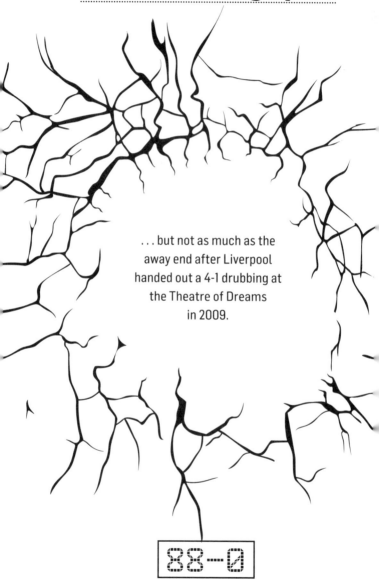

. . . but not as much as the
away end after Liverpool
handed out a 4-1 drubbing at
the Theatre of Dreams
in 2009.

88-0

We Can See You Sneaking Out

Saturday 14 March 2009, Old Trafford, Premier League

United **1**
Ronaldo

v

Liverpool **4**
Torres, Gerrard (pen), Aurelio, Dossena

Old Trafford has become an impregnable fortress and Cristiano Ronaldo puts United ahead from the penalty spot. But the lead lasts just five minutes. Fernando Torres pounces on a mistake by Nemanja Vidic to level the score and Steven Gerrard gives Liverpool the lead on the stroke of half-time with a penalty.

With 15 minutes remaining, Alex Ferguson throws on all his subs. Genius! Liverpool add two more, the first an exquisite free-kick by Fabio Aurelio after Vidic has been sent off, the second a deft lob by sub Andrea Dossena direct from a Pepe Reina clearance. So Liverpool secure a famous double, as does Vidic, who was also sent off in the previous meeting at Anfield.

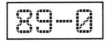

S.W.A.L.K

Stephen Gerrard's very first kiss into the lens at Old Trafford in 2009 has been much imitated but never bettered.

'Top, Top Players'

Yeah, Gerrard's not all that, is he? If only we could have bought the sort of top, top players Ferguson signed, like

~~Djemba-Djemba~~

~~Kléberson~~

~~Bebé~~

~~Bellion~~

~~Obertan~~

~~Verón~~

~~Prunier~~

~~Cruyff~~

~~Carroll~~

~~Bosnich~~

~~Taibi~~

~~Milne~~

So many, you could write a book about them.

Off You Go

See if you can spot the pattern:

September 2008
Liverpool 2 United 1 – Vidic sent off

March 2009
United 1 Liverpool 4 – Vidic sent off

October 2009
Liverpool 2 United 0 – Vidic sent off

March 2013
United 0 Liverpool 3 – Vidic sent off

Yep, whenever Liverpool beat United and
Vidic was playing, he got himself sent off.
On his 13th appearance between the sides
(a 3-0 away win at Old Trafford), Vidic was
sent off for a record fourth time – more than
any other player against a single opponent in
the history of the Premier League.

92–0

Inventive Midfielders

CRAIG JOHNSTON
The Predator boot.
Minibar technology

DAVID BECKHAM
Perfume. Pants

Though both men were equally successful for their clubs, each netting nine major trophies, Koppites will tell you that Beckham wasn't fit to lace Johnston's boots. He did, however, wear them. Beckham's 'wonder goal' against Wimbledon in 1996 and many others were scored thanks to innovative Predator boots invented by Liverpool's Australian winger.

Putting the boot on the other foot, though, it seems unlikely that 'Skippy' would be such a Sheila to wear 'Home by David Beckham' or pull on 'David Beckham Bodywear' pants.

93–0

Taking the Pea

When did simply having your own name on your shirt become so problematic? Maybe it's a Latin thing? If so, it doesn't seem to have registered with Suarez or Coutinho.

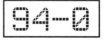

Waving the White Flag

David Moyes – Football Genius

Sunday 16 March 2014, Old Trafford, Premier League

United **0**

v

Liverpool **3**

Gerrard 2, Suarez

'Ten reasons United can beat Liverpool' screams a *Manchester Evening News* feature in the lead-up to this Premier League clash, but on closer inspection it's nothing more than 10 ways in which David Moyes' hapless team need to improve.

They don't. They get worse.

They can't stop giving away penalties. Steven Gerrard puts away the first two and can even afford to hit the post with the third as Nemanja Vidic gets his customary red card and then Luis Suarez finishes the job. Yet another easy three points courtesy of the Moyesiah.

Taking the Mic

*'No one wants to be a full-back
as a kid. No one wants to grow up
and be a Gary Neville.'*

**JAMIE CARRAGHER TAKES AN EARLY LEAD IN
THE BATTLE OF THE PUNDITS ON SKY.**

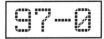

Pep Talk

'I'm happy Liverpool are coming back because they are playing awesome and they deserve to be there.'

PEP GUARDIOLA WELCOMES BACK ENGLAND'S LEADING EUROPEAN CLUB AS UNITED FALL OFF THE UEFA GRAVY TRAIN.

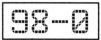

98–0

Theatre of Dreams?

THIS IS ANFIELD

Enough said.

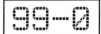

Trump Card

5
3

Oh yes, nearly forgot:
'In Istanbul, we won it FIVE TIMES.'

100--0

TRANSWORLD PUBLISHERS
61–63 Uxbridge Road, London W5 5SA
A Random House Group Company
www.transworldbooks.co.uk

First published in Great Britain
in 2014 by Bantam Press
an imprint of Transworld Publishers

Created and compiled by Will Brooks and Tim Glynne-Jones (United)
copyright © Will Brooks and Tim Glynne-Jones 2014

Design by David Ashford

Visit www.100nil.com for more indefensible screamers.

A CIP catalogue record for this book
is available from the British Library.

ISBN 9780593074596

Addresses for Random House Group Ltd companies outside the UK can be found
at: www.randomhouse.co.uk
The Random House Group Ltd Reg. No. 954009

The Random House Group Limited supports the Forest Stewardship Council®
(FSC®), the leading international forest-certification organisation. Our
books carrying the FSC label are printed on FSC®-certified paper. FSC is the
only forest-certification scheme supported by the leading environmental
organisations, including Greenpeace. Our paper procurement policy can be
found at www.randomhouse.co.uk/environment

Typeset in Flama

Printed and bound in Germany

2 4 6 8 10 9 7 5 3 1

UNITED
100
LIVERPOOL
0

Created and compiled by
Will Brooks and Tim Glynne-Jones

BANTAM PRESS

LONDON · TORONTO · SYDNEY · AUCKLAND · JOHANNESBURG

First

1878
1892

Just a bit more history.

United

A name that reflects the fact that the club was formed through collaboration.
Liverpool was formed out of a dispute with a landlord, probably over fiddling the leckie.

So It Begins

Saturday 2 November 1895, Bank Street, Division Two

Newton Heath **5**
Clarkin, Peters 3, Smith

v

Liverpool **2**
Becton, Ross

Liverpool had joined the Football League in 1893, a year after United (still Newton Heath LYR FC), but, due to a couple of promotions and relegations, the clubs did not meet in the League until 12 October 1895, when Liverpool caught Newton Heath by surprise and secured a lucky win. Three weeks later they face each other again, and this time Newton Heath are taking it seriously. John Clarkin gets the first, followed by a hat-trick for James Peters and a fifth from Dick Smith as Liverpool's bragging rights are cut short after less than a month. In fact, Liverpool will have to wait another nine years for a chance of revenge . . . and then they'll lose again.

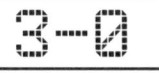

Just a Bit More Famous

While Liverpool have boasted a lot of star names over the years, United's have always been just a bit more famous.

★ UNITED	★ LIVERPOOL
Busby	Shankly
Charlton	Hunt
Best	Keegan
Robson	McMahon
Ferguson	Dalglish
Cantona	Redknapp
Neville	Carragher
Schmeichel	James
Beckham	Gerrard
Rooney	Suarez
Giggs	McManaman

4–0

Just a Few More Fans

354
MILLION[*]

71
MILLION[*]

That's a global fan base five times the size of Liverpool's. And one estimate puts it at 660 million[†]. Even in 1974/75, when United were playing in Division Two, they attracted an average home gate 2,423 bigger than Liverpool in Division One.

Sources: *SPORT+MARKT; †TNS Research International 2011

Just a Bit More Money

£3.3
BILLION

£651
MILLION

The annual Forbes list of most valuable clubs
puts United consistently on top of the world,
with the gap to Liverpool growing year on year.

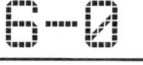

Happy Christmas

Saturday 24 December 1904, Bank Street, Division Two

United **3**

Arkesden, Roberts, Williams

v

Liverpool **1**

Parkinson

Nine years after their previous League
meeting, 40,000 fans gather at Bank Street
on Christmas Eve to see the newly named
Manchester United steam past Liverpool again.
Goals from the prolific Tommy Arkesden,
centre-back Charlie Roberts and 21-year-old
Henry Williams do the damage as Ernest
Mangnall's young side set the trend.

Liverpool 'Football Club'

A Scouser never uses one word when three will do. It's true the spectacle at Anfield might not always be recognizable as football, but is it really necessary to add 'Football Club' on the end every time they talk about Liverpool?

'UNITED'

Says it all.

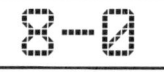

Y.A.W.N

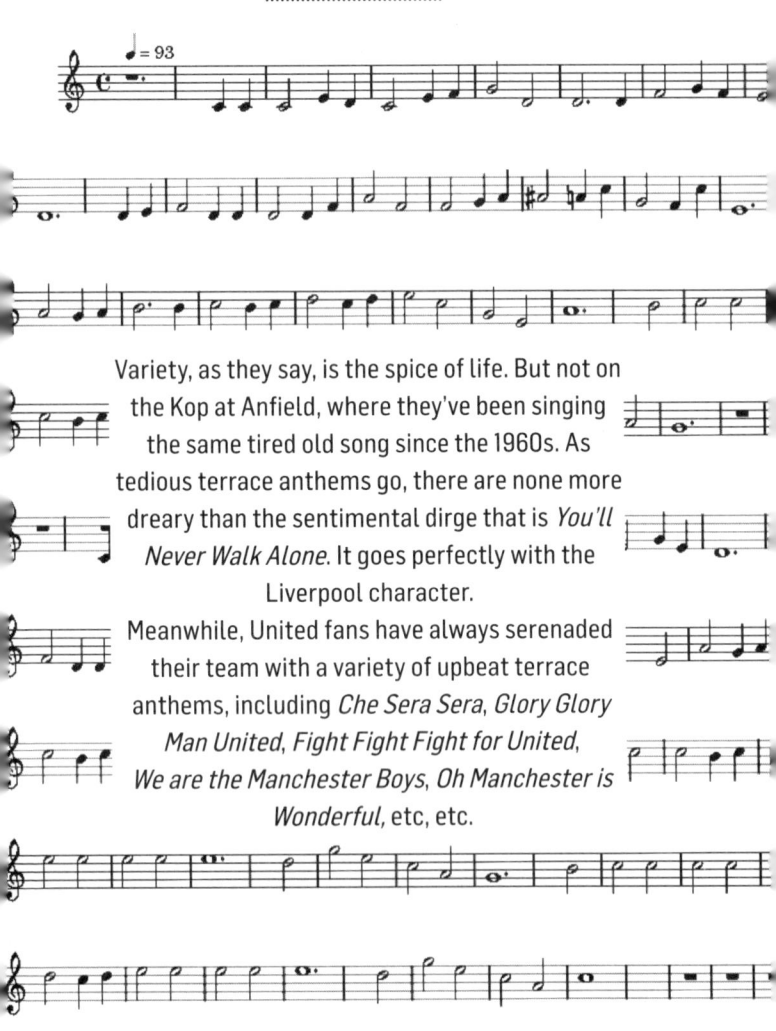

Variety, as they say, is the spice of life. But not on the Kop at Anfield, where they've been singing the same tired old song since the 1960s. As tedious terrace anthems go, there are none more dreary than the sentimental dirge that is *You'll Never Walk Alone*. It goes perfectly with the Liverpool character.

Meanwhile, United fans have always serenaded their team with a variety of upbeat terrace anthems, including *Che Sera Sera*, *Glory Glory Man United*, *Fight Fight Fight for United*, *We are the Manchester Boys*, *Oh Manchester is Wonderful*, etc, etc.

9---0

'When You Walk Through a Storm ...'

February 1986: United players are greeted with a shower of ammonia as they get off the team bus at Anfield. Less than a year after Heysel, Liverpool fans let their club down again.
United have some daft fans, but Liverpool's are always just a bit more stupid.

Another Day, Another Drubbing

Monday 2 September 1907, Bank Street, Division One

United **4**
Turnbull 3, Wall

v

Liverpool **0**

Liverpool are the victims again as a United team featuring such greats as Sandy Turnbull, Charlie Roberts and Billy Meredith make a storming start to the 1907/08 season. Having beaten Aston Villa 4-1 away in the opening fixture, they deal out another four to Liverpool, with a hat-trick for Turnbull and 22-year-old George Wall adding the fourth.

United go on to clinch their first League Championship, averaging more than two goals a game, while Liverpool finish down in eighth place.

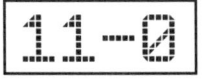

Symbolism

United's symbol is a devil,
representing the dashing, impish
nature of United's style of football.

Liverpool's is a duck.

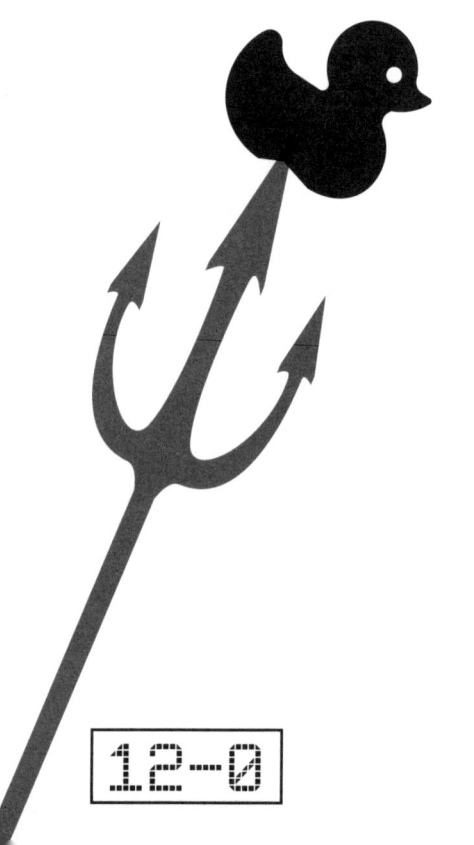

12–0

Steven Gerrard versus . . .
Paul Scholes

SCHOLESIE
European Cups 2

STEVIE G
European Cups 1

13–0

'Hold Your Head Up High . . .'

The replay of Liverpool's ill-fated FA Cup semi-final in 1989 is settled by a cruel own goal by Forest's Brian Laws. John Aldridge reacts with appropriate grace, ruffling Laws' hair and laughing in his face. Nothing to be proud of there.

14–0

Knock Knock

Saturday 1 April 1911, Old Trafford, Division One

United **2**

West 2

v

Liverpool **0**

Liverpool are the April Fools as they suffer their first ever League defeat at United's new home, thanks to two goals from legendary striker Enoch 'Knocker' West in his first season with United. It's a crucial win as United are vying with Aston Villa for the League Championship. They clinch the title by one point with a 5-1 home win against Sunderland on the last day of the season. Liverpool finish 13th.

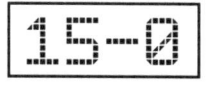

Spiritual Home

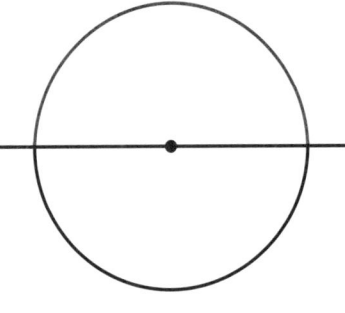

OLD TRAFFORD
Capacity: 75,811
Pitch size: 105m x 68m

ANFIELD
Capacity: 45,522
Pitch size: 101m x 68m

While Anfield is quite a big football ground,
Old Trafford is just a bit bigger.

Strip Tease

United adopted their familiar red shirts, white shorts and black socks when they assumed their famous name in 1902. It took Liverpool another 63 years, mostly spent mimicking United's colours, before they settled on their unimaginative all-red strip.

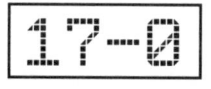

'And Don't Be Afraid
of the Dark . . .'

15 October 2011. Luis Suarez, the Uruguayan
striker Liverpool bought after seeing him sent off
against Ghana in the World Cup for cheating, calls
United left-back Patrice Evra 'negro' during an
altercation in a 1-1 draw at Anfield. Suarez later
claims his meaning had been lost in translation.
The FA don't agree and ban him for eight games,
along with a £40,000 fine.

18—0

Make Mine a Double

Saturday 29 March 1913, Anfield, Division One

Liverpool **0**

v

United **2**

Wall, West

After a 3-1 home victory earlier in the season, United travel to Anfield in hope of securing their first ever double over Liverpool. They achieve it thanks to goals from George Wall and Knocker West. The win, though, is largely down to United's defence, who stop Liverpool scoring for only the second time in their meetings at Anfield. It's United's 15th clean sheet in a season that will see them keep 17 in all out of 38 games, on their way to finishing fourth, eight places above Liverpool.

'At the End of the Storm . . .'

'I think you're bang out of order to blame Luis Suarez for anything that happened here today.'

Kenny Dalglish makes a fool of himself on national television, having a go at Sky reporter Geoff Shreeves after Suarez's refusal to shake Patrice Evra's hand at Old Trafford throws more fuel onto an already explosive racial dispute between the clubs.
Dalglish is later forced to apologize, as is Suarez for his 'mistake'.

20–0

The Lingering Taste of Defeat

The name of United's famous Stretford End serves as a constant reminder to visiting teams of where they are. Liverpool's Kop is a constant reminder of defeat. It takes its name from the Spion Kop, a hill in South Africa where the British army was massacred during the Boer War. Nice choice.

Still, what was the alternative?
The Everton End?

21–0

Shipping Goals

Liverpool was a thriving port until the Manchester
merchants decided to cut the overcharging
Scousers out of the operation and bring the cargo
right up to their doorstep.
The Manchester Ship Canal remains a thorn in
Liverpool's side to this day and United's badge
serves as a constant reminder.

Flood Gates

Saturday 5 May 1928, Old Trafford, Division One

United **6**

Hanson, Rawlings 2, Spence 3

v

Liverpool **1**

Hodgson

Like the lid being blown off a pressure cooker, this record win comes on the last day of a poor season for United. A difficult period for the club is forgotten as they rattle six past Liverpool keeper Arthur Riley. It's particularly satisfying for hat-trick hero Joe Spence, a loyal servant, who had been at the club throughout those barren years.

Record Attendance

76,962

61,905

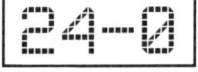

'A Golden Sky . . .'

May 1977. Liverpool fans turn out in their
thousands to celebrate winning the European
Cup. On the balcony of St George's Hall, the
players are in high spirits. Terry McDermott feels
the call of nature, but instead of going and finding
a toilet, he decides to urinate off the balcony,
on to a group of nurses standing below.
United players don't urinate on their own fans,
or those of any other club.

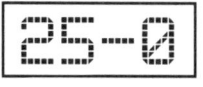

Normal Service Resumed

Wednesday 11 Sep 1946, Maine Road, Division One

United **5**

Mitten, Pearson 3, Rowley

v

Liverpool **0**

Having signed off before the war with a 2-0 win over Liverpool, United resume hostilities with a 5-0 thumping. Among Liverpool's number is future manager Bob Paisley, but it's ex-Liverpool player Matt Busby who masterminds this rout, the 37-year-old recently installed as United manager. Forced to play home games at Manchester City's Maine Road ground while the bomb-damaged Old Trafford is rebuilt, United show all the signs of a great side in the making, local lad Stan Pearson doing the bulk of the damage with a hat-trick, sandwiched between goals for Charlie Mitten and Jack Rowley.

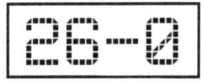

'The Sweet Silver Song of a Lark . . .'

Not at all friendly
Not at all trustworthy
Not at all intelligent

The Scouse accent came out top in all these
categories in a 2013 ComRes poll carried out for
ITV's *Tonight* programme.
The Manchester accent performed at least twice
as favourably in all three categories.

27–0

Busby's Aces

Saturday 24 January 1948, Goodison Park, FA Cup

United **3**

Mitten, Morris, Rowley

v

Liverpool **0**

74,000 at Goodison Park for an FA Cup fourth-round tie. Champions Liverpool are the next obstacle on United's march to Wembley for their first trophy under Matt Busby. Some obstacle. United run out comfortable winners and go on to win the cup 4-2 against Blackpool.

FA Cup

While Liverpool have a reasonable FA Cup
record, United have won it just a few times more,
including two final victories over Liverpool,
in 1977 and 1996.

Gillette

For longstanding United fans, that name means 'the old one-two', Doc, Steve Coppell and Gordon Hill advertising razor blades. For Liverpool fans it means being ridden hard from behind by a cowboy.

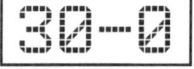

30–0

'Walk on Through the Wind . . .'

'I've been driven out.' An Anfield local reacts to Liverpool's campaign of buying up local houses and leaving them empty as part of their plan to expand the stadium. They even spent years trying to drive two elderly sisters, Joan and Nora Mason, out of their home in Kemlyn Road. Two decades of dereliction have driven down house prices, turned the area into a slum and left residents with no choice but to sell up cheap. 'The people's club', Shankly called it.

While Liverpool's expansion plans have stalled for years, United have turned Old Trafford into a magnificent, modern stadium. And they've done it without making anyone homeless.

31–0

Byrne's Night

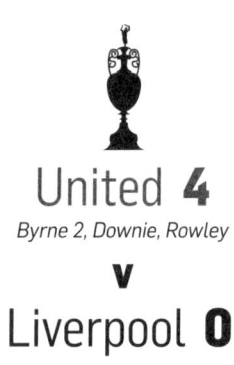

United **4**

Byrne 2, Downie, Rowley

v

Liverpool **0**

The name Roger Byrne is enshrined in United legend and this is the season his United career begins. The inspiring full-back from Gorton, who makes a record 33 consecutive appearances for England and captains the Busby Babes from 1953 until his death at Munich aged just 28, will become one of the greatest defenders the English game has ever seen. But he begins as a winger and the two goals he scores in this drubbing of Liverpool come in a purple patch that sees him score seven in the last six games of the season to help United to the title. John Downie and Jack Rowley complete the rout.

FA Youth Cup

Home Grown

Liverpool tend to buy
success, whereas
United breed it.
United had nine home-
grown players in the team that won their first
European Cup in 1968. Liverpool had four in 1977.
In 1999 when United won it again, they had
four in the starting line-up, four
on the bench and one
(Paul Scholes)
suspended. In 2005
Liverpool had two.

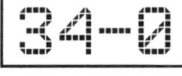

'Walk on Through the Rain . . .'

If you're going to dish out retribution to a fan who's out of order, a flying kung-fu kick and a couple of swings are the United way, as demonstrated by Eric Cantona at Selhurst Park.

The Liverpool way is to spit on them, as demonstrated by El Hadji Diouf at Celtic Park in 2003.

Sweet Sorrow

Saturday 19 December 1953, Old Trafford, Division One

United **5**

Blanchflower 2, Taylor 2, Violett

v

Liverpool **1**

Bimpson

The rivalry is about to undergo another forced intermission as United's and Liverpool's fortunes take very different turns. The United team sheet reads like a roll call of legends: Ray Wood, Bill Foulkes, Roger Byrne, Jeff Whitefoot, Allenby Chilton, Duncan Edwards, Johnny Berry, Jackie Blanchflower, Tommy Taylor, Dennis Viollet, Jack Rowley. Chilton and Rowley apart, the average age is just 21, including a 17-year-old Duncan Edwards. Liverpool can't live with them. In fact, they can't live with anybody this season, so they go down, bottom of the league, and they won't be back for another eight years.

First in Europe

1956
1964

United beat Liverpool into Europe by eight years, standing up to the orders of the Football League to become the first English club to play in the European Cup.

United were the first English club to win it too, in 1968, nine years earlier than Liverpool.

And when Liverpool fans got English clubs banned from Europe for five years in the 80s, United led them back, winning the Cup Winners' Cup in 1991 v Barcelona in Rotterdam.

37—0

Soap Wars

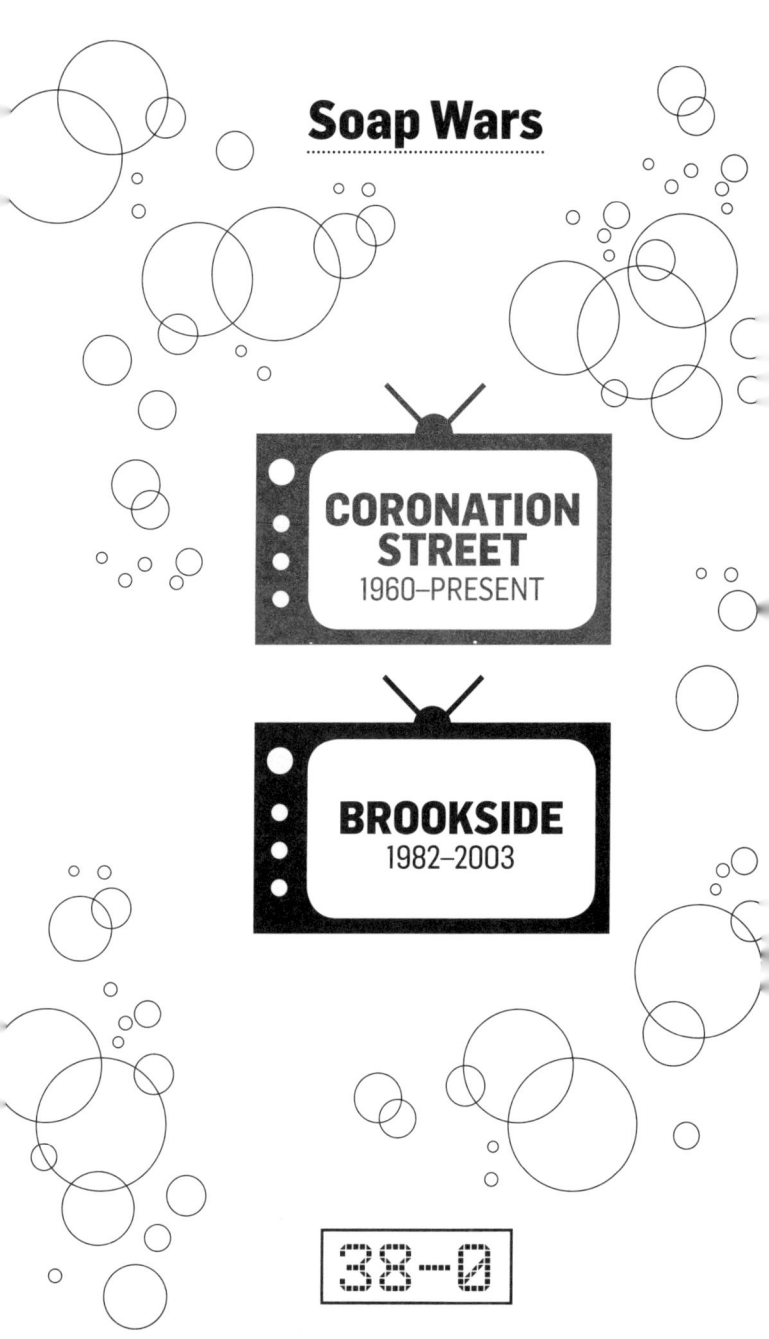

CORONATION STREET
1960–PRESENT

BROOKSIDE
1982–2003

38–0

'Though Your Dreams Be Tossed and Blown...'

Sex toys, strippers and the Spice Boys. The *Independent* described the Liverpool team's 1998 get-together as 'the most debauched Christmas party ever to shame soccer'.
Fowler, McManaman, Redknapp, McAteer, Carragher and Ruddock were a bunch of relatively talented players, but their off-field desires were stronger than their dreams of winning trophies for Liverpool. Wouldn't have happened at a proper football club.

39–0

The Rivalry Builds

Liverpool 0

v

United 2
Crerend, Herd

After eight years in Division Two, Liverpool have come back up under a new manager, Bill Shankly, and won the title in their second season back. Meanwhile, Busby's third great team is taking shape. The rivalry is reaching boiling point. The clubs will take turns to win the title between 1964 and 1967. A new bunch of legends in the making lines up against champions Liverpool at Anfield on this Halloween afternoon: Brennan, Crerand, Stiles, Charlton, Herd, Law, Best . . . and 12 years after his debut, 32-year-old Bill Foulkes. A rare goal for captain Paddy Crerand sets United on their way and a second from David Herd seals this victory in Shankly's 'fortress'.

They Played for Both Sides *Part I*

JOHN PHILIP CHISNALL

John Philip Chisnall holds the distinction of being the last player to be transferred directly between United and Liverpool, way back in 1964. A 22-year-old inside-forward who had made 35 senior appearances and scored eight goals, Chisnall looked like another promising talent coming out of the Busby stable at Old Trafford. Promising enough for Bill Shankly to pay £25,000 for him.

It wasn't Shankly's finest hour. In fact, as transfers go, he made Andy Carroll look like good business. At Liverpool he played six games in three years and scored one goal, before being offloaded to Southend. Chuckle.

'Walk On, Walk On . . .'

One of the charms of going to Anfield is having to park your car or coach miles from the ground and then paying off the local scallies so they won't nick your wheels, because the club has no parking facilities for fans.
Old Trafford has 11 car parks, as befits a 21st-century football club.

Steven Gerrard versus . . .
Roy Keane

KEANO

STEVIE G

It's the Law

United **3**

Conelly, Law 2

v

Liverpool **0**

The last week of the season sees United vying with Leeds for the title with three games to play. The Yorkies are one point ahead but only have two games left. Outgoing champions Liverpool are out of contention but still pose a major threat to United's title ambitions. After John Connelly opens the scoring, Denis Law strikes twice to delight the crowd of 55,772. Two days later, United clinch the title with a 3-1 win over Arsenal. Liverpool finish seventh.

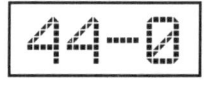

'With Hope in Your Heart . . .'

Bill Shankly was made welcome by
Tommy Docherty at Old Trafford after
he retired as manager of Liverpool.
Sadly, the club he rescued from oblivion
couldn't extend him the same courtesy.

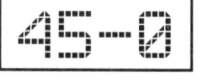

Heroes of '66

United had Bobby Charlton and Nobby Stiles;
Liverpool had Roger Hunt, the striker who
forgot to put the ball in the back of the net in
a World Cup final.

46–0

Leaders

Only four players have won more than
50 caps as captain of England.
Two of them played for United.

Bryan Robson **65**
David Beckham **59**

None of them played for Liverpool.

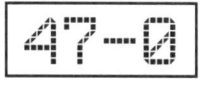

Simply the Best

Liverpool **1**

Hunt

v

United **2**

Best 2

Armistice Day, but there is no peace at Anfield as 54,515 fans roar on the two best teams in the country. The previous season has seen two draws between the sides on the way to United reclaiming the title but here the deadlock is broken by George Best, whose two goals in this game mean he's scored five of United's last seven goals against Liverpool (Denis Law getting the other two). Although Roger Hunt replies late on for Liverpool, it's United who go away with the points. Neither team will win the League this year, as Manchester City are given a rare taste of success. United finish second, a point clear of Liverpool in third, but more importantly end the season as European Champions, the first English club to achieve that honour.

Most Appearances

963
RYAN
GIGGS

857
IAN
CALLAGHAN

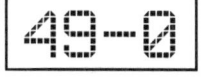

Christmas Comes Early

Saturday 13 December 1969, Anfield, Division One

Liverpool **1**
Hughes

v

United **4**
Yeats (og), Ure, Morgan, Charlton

The season is barely half way through and already United are securing a glorious double over Liverpool. They take the lead with a scrappy own goal from a Bobby Charlton corner before Emlyn Hughes equalizes. Ian Ure restores United's lead early in the second half and Willie Morgan extends it. He then plays a lovely one-two with Charlton, who rifles the ball past Tommy Lawrence into the top right corner to give United a resounding victory to round off a glorious decade.

Famous Fans

UNITED	LIVERPOOL
Morrissey *(charming man)*	Kilroy *(smarmy git)*
Bryn Terfel *(bass-baritone)*	Cilla Black *(base monotone)*
Gary Rhodes *(hotpot)*	Muammar Gaddafi *(despot)*
Albert Finney *(classy)*	Adam Woodyatt *(soapy)*
Sean Connery *(best Bond)*	Daniel Craig *(second-best Bond)*
Usain Bolt *(world's fastest man)*	Yohan Blake *(world's second-fastest man)*

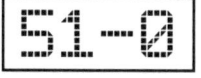

This is Anfield

Liverpool fans are renowned for the sporting way in which they welcome visitors to Anfield. A famous picture of a United fan at Anfield in 1978 with a dart sticking out of his nose perfectly captures this unique hospitality.
In their defence, they were going for the Treble but missed.

Skip to My Lou

Saturday 21 May 1977, Wembley Stadium, FA Cup Final

United **2**

Pearson, J Greenhoff

v

Liverpool **1**

Case

Liverpool have just won the League and four days later they will face Borussia Mönchengladbach in the European Cup Final. An historic 'treble' is theirs for the taking. Surely no club could be so mighty as to win a 'treble' of League, FA Cup and European Cup, could they? Well, yes they could, but not for another 22 years, and then it would be United, not Liverpool, making history. Liverpool's dream ends in five madcap minutes. Stuart Pearson slams United ahead with a trademark screamer, Jimmy Case equalizes two minutes later, and then Lou Macari mishits a shot that hits Jimmy Greenhoff and deflects past Ray Clemence to give United the win. Beautiful in so many ways.

Charity Shield

United

Liverpool

No friendlies at this level.

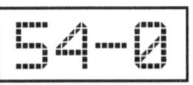

Robbed

Such was the regularity of burglaries in Liverpool players' houses that in 2009 Paddy Power started offering odds on who'd be next. It would help if they didn't keep leaving the back door wide open. United players are more secure, but then they've got all those winners' medals to think about.

55–0

The Master Craftsman

United **1**
J Greenhoff

v

Liverpool **0**

If anyone ever asks you to define the classic English cup tie, point them to this game. Four days after drawing 2-2 in another classic at Maine Road, the teams meet again in front of 53,069 at Goodison Park. Liverpool are the dominant team in England, but United have a few legendary names of their own, including Jimmy Greenhoff – 'the master craftsman'. With 13 minutes to go, after 167 breathless minutes of vintage cup-tie football, Mickey Thomas tricks his way into the Liverpool area and delivers a cross that bounces onto Greenhoff's head for a neatly taken goal. It's enough to settle the tie. On the final whistle, both sets of coaches embrace. Football is the winner. Well, football and United . . .

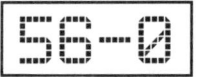

Steven Gerrard versus . . .
David Beckham

BECKS
England Captain **59 times**

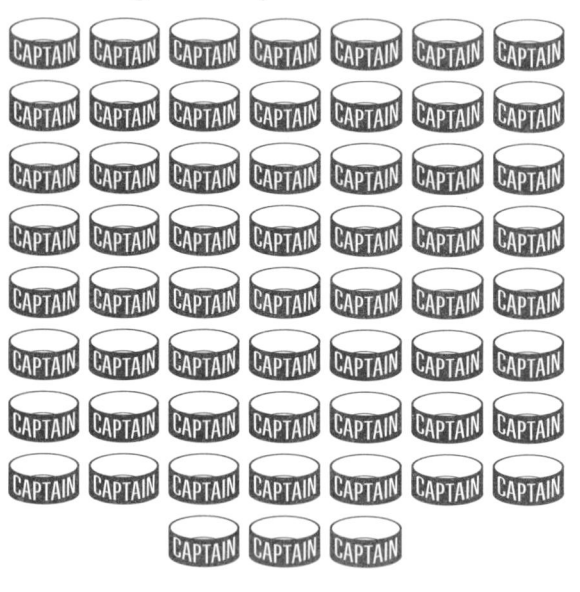

STEVIE G
England Captain **38 times**

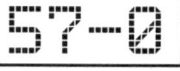

57–0

Twelve Years, 24 Games

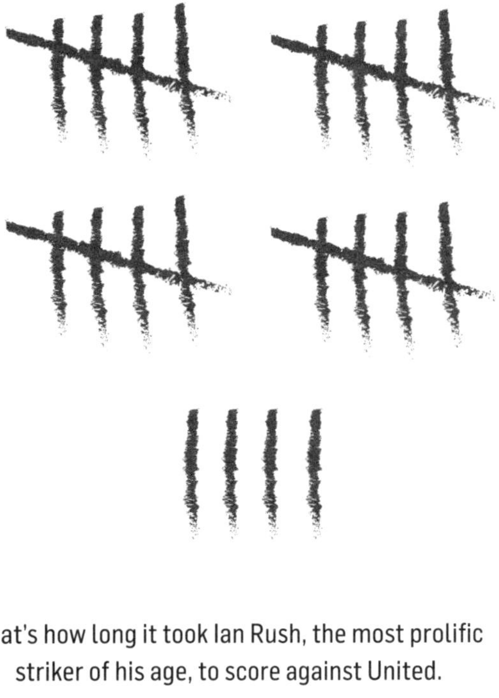

That's how long it took Ian Rush, the most prolific striker of his age, to score against United.

58-0

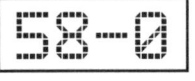

If You Only Win One Away Game All Season . . .

Friday 26 December 1986, Anfield, Division One

Liverpool **0**

v

United **1**

Whiteside

Boxing Day, one month and 20 days into the reign of new manager Alex Ferguson. Fergie has pledged to 'knock Liverpool right off their perch', instantly tapping into the hatred that has seen the United team attacked with ammonia as they got off the bus at Anfield the previous February. To help ensure safe passage, former Liverpool boss Bob Paisley travels on the United bus this time. Norman Whiteside scores the only goal of the game for United's only away win of the season and it's first blood to Fergie in the ongoing clash with Kenny Dalglish.

Doubles

Liverpool may have done it first but United have done it just a few times more.

(United won the Double that season.)

19 August 1995
ALAN HANSEN
'You'll win nothing with kids.'

One-Eyed Pundits

You want impartiality? Don't ask an
ex-Liverpool player. From Ian 'I can't see
past Liverpool' St John to Jamie 'I think
Liverpool will win it now' Carragher, via
Alan 'You'll win nothing with kids' Hansen
and Mark 'Absolutely, Gary' Lawrenson,
they just don't seem to get what the point
of a pundit is.
If you want unsentimental objectivity,
Gary Neville and Roy Keane are the go-to
ex-pros.

It's got to be Gordon

Monday 4 April 1988, Anfield, Division One

Liverpool **3**
Beardsley, Gillespie, McMahon

v

United **3**
Robson 2, Strachan

Despite a controversial red card for Colin
Gibson, Liverpool still can't find a way past Alex
Ferguson's United. 3-2 up and cruising to the
final whistle, they are undone by a mazy dribble
from Gordon Strachan, who slots the ball past
Bruce Grobbelaar before strolling in front of the
irate Koppites smoking an imaginary cigar. So
much cooler than kissing cameras.

Bum Rap

COME ON YOU REDS
Status Quo – Number 1

ANFIELD RAP
Derek B and Craig Johnston – Number 3

United have been responsible for their fair share of bad Cup Final songs, but the *Anfield Rap*? Please . . .
At least United's songs were usually backed up by winning the Cup. *Anfield Rap* will forever remain the soundtrack for the unforgettable comedy that was Liverpool 0 Wimbledon 1. *Come On You Reds* is the only club song to go to Number 1.

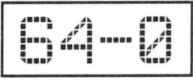

Cowboys

Tom Hicks and George Gillett took
Liverpool for a ride over a period of three
years, which, fortunately for the Scousers,
didn't interfere with their success, since
they weren't having any anyway.
When Michael Knighton rode into Old
Trafford and tried to juggle his way to
power, he was chased out of town before
his balls could touch the ground.

65--0

Happy New Year

Sunday 1 January 1989, Old Trafford, Division One

United **3**

McClair, Hughes, Beardsmore

v

Liverpool **1**

Barnes

Six years before Alan Hansen famously doubts the value of youth, United prove that you can win a steamy New Year's Day clash against the Scousers with kids. Liverpool are going for the title and are expected to turn United over, especially after John Barnes puts them ahead with 20 minutes to go. But a United team inspired by Russell Beardsmore (20), Lee Sharpe (17), Lee Martin (20) and sub Mark Robins (19) fights back with three dramatic goals from Brian McClair, Mark Hughes and finally Beardsmore, who strokes a Sharpe cross home at the far post to confirm an unforgettable win.

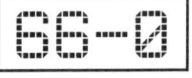

GARY PALLISTER
GLENN HYSEN

Glenn Hysén could have had it all. In 1989 United agreed a deal to sign him from Fiorentina for £300,000. He might have been part of the team that won title after title in the 90s but he backed out of the deal and chose Liverpool. United signed Pally instead. The rest is history.

	Gary Pallister	Glenn Hysén
League title	4	1
FA Cup	3	0
League Cup	1	0
UEFA Cup Winners' Cup	1	0
UEFA Super Cup	1	0

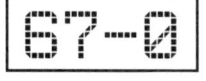

Calm Down, Calm Down

Liverpool is the most ridiculed city in England. From the *Liver Birds* to *Bread* to Harry Enfield's Scousers, we've all been laughing at Liverpool for decades. People tend to take Manchester a bit more seriously.

Steven Gerrard versus . . .
Ryan Giggs

GIGGSY
Seasons 24

STEVIE G
Seasons 17

69–0

Chocs Away!

Liverpool **1**
Rush

v

United **2**
Hughes, McClair

United take a major step towards their first Premiership title with this win at Anfield. The era of United dominance is about to begin, as Liverpool's star flickers and dies. Mark Hughes gives United the lead just before half-time but Ian Rush equalizes five minutes into the second half. But there'll be no choking from United, and they respond with a headed goal from Brian 'Choccy' McClair six minutes later to clinch three vital points.

They Played for
Both Sides *Part II*

PAUL EMERSON
CARLYLE INCE
aka 'The Guvnor'. Well, he was for United.

	United	Liverpool
League title	2	0
FA Cup	2	0
League Cup	1	0
European Cup Winners' Cup	1	0
European Super Cup	1	0
Charity Shield	3	0

The player Fergie branded a 'Big-Time Charlie'
seemed to lose his mojo when he crossed the
threshold at Anfield. Strange.

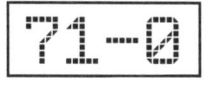

Crowning Moment

For most clubs, an invitation to the Palace should be the easy way to pick up a title. 5 May 2014: Liverpool's collapse at Selhurst Park after holding a 3-0 lead with 12 minutes to go leaves their dreams in tatters for yet another year.

Flashback to 21 April 1993: United go to Crystal Palace needing a win to give them the edge over Aston Villa in the title chase. A comfortable 2-0 victory does the job.

Neil Before the King

When Eric Cantona made his return after being
banned for fighting a fascist at Selhurst Park,
his first game at Anfield saw him up against
leg-breaker Neil Ruddock, and Ruddock was out
to wind him up. Ruddock's ploy was to turn Eric's
collar down, an act that went unseen by the TV
cameras. What the world did see was Eric doing
a fantastic impression of Ruddock: the fat belly
and saggy chin.
Oh, and then Eric scored.

73-0

White Suits, White Flag

Saturday 11 May 1996, Wembley Stadium, FA Cup Final

United **1**

Cantona

v

Liverpool **0**

The second time United meet Liverpool in the Cup Final and the second time they beat them. In 1977 Liverpool were going for an historic Treble. This time United are going for an historic second Double. Where Liverpool failed, United will succeed. White suits. Spice boys. That's Liverpool. Champions. Kids. That's United, with Cantona the genius uncle. Captain for the day, 13 days short of his 30th birthday, he will become the first non-British player to lift the FA Cup as captain, having secured that second Double for United with an amazing strike from the edge of the area that finds its way past seven Liverpool defenders and the prone David James.

Video Games

'I was getting carried away playing Tekken II and Tomb Raider for hours on end.'

After a 3-0 defeat to Newcastle, Liverpool keeper David 'Calamity' James sheds some light on the secret of success at Anfield in the 90s. While Liverpool players got addicted to video games, United players starred in them.

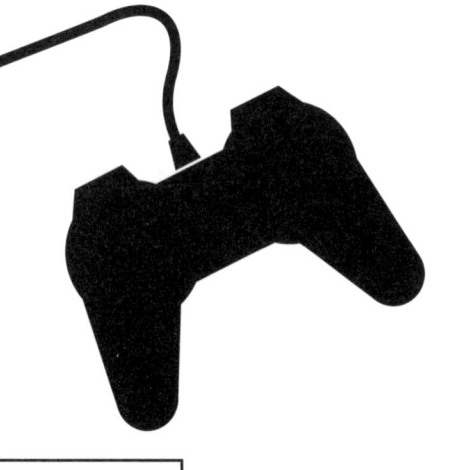

75-0

The Treble

Liverpool will tell you they've done it twice, but their Mickey Mouse trebles in 1984 and 2001 included the League Cup on both occasions and the UEFA Cup second time around.
Not quite good enough, sorry.
United are the only club to win the proper Treble of League Championship, FA Cup and European Cup.

Ole Ole Ole Ole

Sunday 24 January 1999, Old Trafford, FA Cup fourth round

United **2**
Yorke, Solskjaer

v

Liverpool **1**
Owen

It's the season of late, late goals, of Dwight Yorke and Andy Cole, of Teddy Sheringham and Ole Gunnar Solskjaer. 1998/99, United's Treble winning season, and on the way comes this peach of a late turnaround to knock Liverpool out of the FA Cup. Michael Owen (long before his salvation) puts the visitors ahead after just three minutes and they dig in for a further 85.

But oh, they haven't read the script. With two minutes remaining, Cole nods down and Yorke taps in to set up a nail-biting finale. United love nail-biting finales and sure enough, two minutes later Solskjaer breaks Scouse hearts with a clinical left-foot finish and United's march to the Treble gathers momentum.

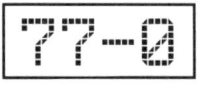

Knight Games

Sir Matt Busby

Sir Bobby Charlton

Sir Alex Ferguson

Mr Bill Shankly, Mr Ian St John and
Mr Kenny Dalglish did not make it into
Her Majesty's dream team.

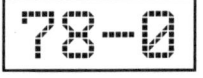

Oh Gee!

Jamie Carragher stands second in the all-time list of Premiership own-goal scorers with seven, topped only by Richard Dunne of City fame with nine. Carragher's brace in United's 3-2 win at Anfield in 1999 were the perfect punch line to round off a century of laughs. Thanks, Jamie. It's been a pleasure.

Play Acting

Many many years ago, back when Liverpool were good, players like Graeme Souness, Ian Rush and Kenny Dalglish were forever turning up with embarrassing cameo appearances in any TV drama with a passing reference to Merseyside.

United's stars have been happy to focus on their football, leaving the movie moghuls to name films after them (*Bend It Like Beckham*), or wait till they retired before winning proper roles in proper films (*Waiting for Eric*).

80–0

Ruudy Can't Fail

Saturday 5 April 2003, Old Trafford, Premiership

United **4**

Van Nistelrooy 2, Giggs, Solskjaer

v

Liverpool **0**

United reinforce their superiority in emphatic style during a run-in to the title that sees them win nine of their last 10 games, averaging just under three goals a game. So this result is no great surprise. Nor is the identity of the scorer of United's first two goals. Ruud Van Nistelrooy is banging them in for fun and will finish the season with 44 goals to his name. Sami Hyypia gets sent off after five minutes, Liverpool dig in for an hour, but United take them apart with further goals from Ryan Giggs and Ole Gunnar Solskjaer.

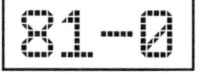

Mawkish Sentimentality

Boris Johnson may have gone a bit far in his
Spectator critique of Merseyside, but he wasn't
wrong in noticing that the image of the chirpy
Scouser seems to have given way to something
more downbeat since 1990.
United fans are just a bit happier.

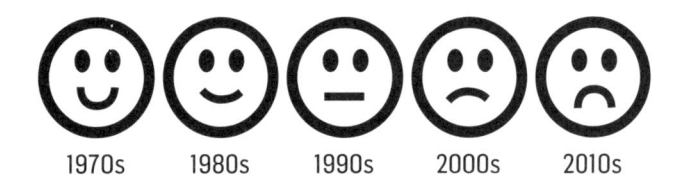

1970s   1980s   1990s   2000s   2010s

One-Club Man

Steve Gerrard, Gerrard
He kisses the badge on his chest
Then hands in a transfer request
Steve Gerrard, Gerrard

Liverpool's title-less legend may never have left his boyhood club, but not for want of trying. You didn't see Bobby Charlton or Ryan Giggs angling for a move to Chelsea. But then, with 16 titles between them, they didn't need to look around.

You're Not Singing Any More

Saturday 15 January 2005, Anfield, Premiership

Liverpool **0**

v

United **1**

Rooney

It's been nearly eight years since United did the double over Liverpool, a period in which they have won the title five times. Now, in the middle of a three-year break from being champions, United turn their attentions away from Arsenal and Chelsea for a moment to put Liverpool back in their box. Wayne Rooney, the 19-year-old prodigy from Croxteth, has been signed from Everton at the start of the season and is looking for his first ever goal against Liverpool to silence the Kop, who single him out for special treatment from the start. After 21 minutes, he takes a short pass from Cristiano Ronaldo and unleashes a shot from 25 yards that dips under Jerzy Dudek and into the net. Sing up, Scousers. We can't hear you.

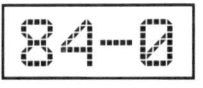

It Started With a Kiss

Steven Gerrard's love affair
with the camera began when he
scored at Old Trafford, and was played
out embarrassingly in public for several
years. But it ended in a messy divorce
at Selhurst Park, the broken-hearted
Stevie G publicly pushing his beloved
lens away as Liverpool's 2014 title
dream went down the tube.
What a choker.

85–0

PFA Player of the Year

11

6

Liverpool players have won a fair number
of PFA Player of the Year awards, but
United have won just a few more.

Fore!

A bit of healthy rivalry within a first-team squad is par for the course but whacking a teammate with a golf club is strictly out of bounds. Step forward Craig Bellamy, the 'Pride of Merseyside'.

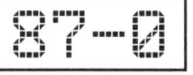

O'Sssshea

Saturday 3 March 2007, Anfield, Premiership

Liverpool **0**

v

United **1**
O'Shea

Another victory, another double, another last-minute winner from a United defender ... and another title in the bag for United, as they go on to secure their ninth Premiership triumph by six points. Liverpool finish third, a mere 19 points behind. It's not looking good when Paul Scholes gets sent off for taking a swing at Xabi Alonso, but United are not prepared to settle for a draw and in the 90th minute, seconds after Edwin van der Sar has made a fantastic save from Peter Crouch, a Cristiano Ronaldo free kick falls to John O'Shea, who sweeps the ball into the roof of the net to silence the Kop and send United on their way to glory.

They (Almost) Played For Both Sides

Gabriel Heinze seemed like a pretty smart left-back when he came to United in 2004. He looked like a United player, scored on his debut and was voted United's Player of the Year in his first season. He went on to win the Premiership and League Cup, but there was obviously something he didn't understand. Because in the summer of 2007, he put in a request for a transfer to Liverpool.

It wasn't the 60s any more. You just didn't do that sort of thing. And with two years left on his contract, United blocked the move. Liverpool manager Rafa Benítez was prepared to pay £6.8million and get lawyers involved. United held firm. And Heinze got his move . . . to Real Madrid.

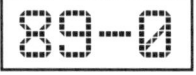

Rafa's Cracking Up

January 2009, Liverpool are sitting on top of the League and Rafa Benítez is asked about comments Alex Ferguson has made about the fixture list. He produces a piece of paper from his pocket and proceeds to reel off a catalogue of accusations about the conduct of his United counterpart.

'I want to talk about facts. I want to be clear. I do not want to play mind games too early, although they seem to want to start.'

What he doesn't realize is that the mind games have already started and he has walked right into the trap. Liverpool draw their next three games and manage only two wins in seven, while United embark on a run of nine straight wins. They can even afford a 4-1 defeat at Anfield as they total 17 victories out of their last 20 matches to beat Liverpool to the title by four points.

And that's a fact.

90-0

Dimi Three

Sunday 19 September 2010, Old Trafford, Premiership

United **3**
Berbatov 3

v

Liverpool **2**
Gerrard 2

A five-goal thriller featuring two goalscorers: Liverpool talisman Steven Gerrard and United's mercurial Bulgarian Dimitar Berbatov. Berbatov sets things in motion just before half-time with a clever header, and adds a second with an adept overhead kick on the hour. But Gerrard drags Liverpool back with a penalty and a free-kick in six minutes. The momentum is with the visitors so with eight minutes to go, Alex Ferguson throws on a third striker, Federico Macheda. It works. Two minutes later, John O'Shea sends in a cross that Berbatov heads home to become the first United player since Stan Pearson in 1946 to score a hat-trick against Liverpool. United will also go on to break Liverpool's record of 18 titles.

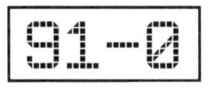

They Played for
Both Sides *Part III*

MICHAEL
OWEN

Liverpool's brightest home-grown player of the modern era was given a run out at United in the twilight of his career. A bit-part player blighted by injury, his United highlights amounted to a hat-trick in the Champions League and a famous winner against City, but his stats make interesting reading.

	Appearances	Titles
United	31	1
Liverpool	216	0

Stirred But Not Shaken

Saturday 11 February 2012, Old Trafford, Premiership

United **2**
Rooney 2

v

Liverpool **1**
Suarez

There are rivalries and there are bitter rivalries. This game is cloaked in bitterness before it even kicks off. The previous League encounter in October has been marred by Liverpool's Luis Suarez racially abusing Patrice Evra. Everyone in football has been outraged, with the exception of Kenny Dalglish, back in charge of the Anfield boot room. After months of acrimony, this game is supposed to lay it all to rest with a handshake between the two players. Suarez shuns the gesture and the bitterness swells. He scores late on, but only after Wayne Rooney has bagged two in five minutes after the break to give United the points, and secure the stage for Evra to whip up the Stretford End as Suarez trudges from the pitch.

His Teeth Are Offside

Luis Suarez gets a mouthful from
the Stretford End.

94-0

BUBBLE PERMS, PORN-STAR 'TACHES, SHELL SUITS, AMATEUR RAPS, MILK ADS, WHITE SUITS . . .

Where Liverpool leads, the world falls about.

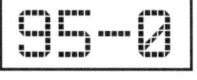

Steven Gerrard versus . . .
Luke Chadwick

LUKE
Titles **1**

STEVIE G
Titles **0**

Peace, Love and Harmony

Sunday 23 September 2012, Anfield, Premiership

Liverpool **1**
Gerrard

v

United **2**
Rafael, Van Persie

In complete contrast to the previous fixture, this game is played in an atmosphere of relative goodwill, prompted by the recent publication of the independent report into the Hillsborough Disaster. Floral tributes from both clubs set the tone, aided by a handshake between Patrice Evra and Luis Suarez. Kenny Dalglish is gone too, replaced by Brendan Rodgers, and when Jonjo Shelvey gets himself sent off in the first half, the Anfield hospitality is looking impeccable. Steven Gerrard spoils it briefly with a goal just after half-time, but Rafael da Silva equalizes five minutes later with a sweet left-foot strike and new boy Robin Van Persie settles the win from the spot in the last 10 minutes. Happy days.

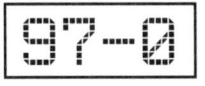

After All That

2013/14 was Liverpool's
best season for 24 years
and had them dreaming
of winning the title for the
first time since 1990. It was
United's worst season in
the same period and they
finished up with nothing.
So did Liverpool.

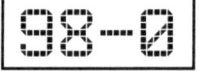

Head to Head

By the end of 2013/14, after 120 years of playing each other, United held the balance of power by a clear 11 wins in all competitions. With eight more wins in the League and three more in the cups, Liverpool still have a lot of catching up to do.

Titles

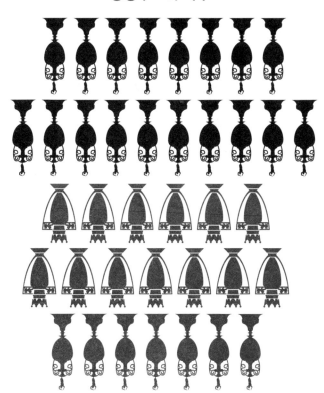

United 20
Liverpool 18

While Liverpool have won a lot of titles,
United have won just a couple more.

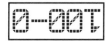